FORGET
NOT

H S

BENEFITS

FORGET
NOT
H S

BENEFITS

ROBERTS LIARDON

Banner
Publishing

Unless otherwise indicated, all Scripture quotations are taken
from the King James Version of the Holy Bible. Scripture
quotations marked (NKJV) are taken from the *New King James
Version*, © 1979, 1980, 1982, 1984 by Thomas Nelson, Inc. Used
by permission. All rights reserved.

Boldface type in the Scripture quotations indicates the author's
emphasis.

FORGET NOT HIS BENEFITS

Roberts Liardon Ministries
P.O. Box 2989
Sarasota, FL 34230
E-mail: info1@robertsliardon.org
www.RobertsLiardon.com

ISBN: 978-1-62911-225-1
eBook ISBN: 978-1-62911-226-8
Printed in the United States of America
© 1993, 2014 by Roberts Liardon

Distributed by
Banner Publishing
1030 Hunt Valley Circle
New Kensington, PA 15068

1 2 3 4 5 6 7 8 9 10 ẞ 20 19 18 17 16 15 14

CONTENTS

Introduction 9

1. Bless the Lord 17

2. Forgetting the Past 37

3. Forget Not All His Benefits 57

About the Author 87

INTRODUCTION

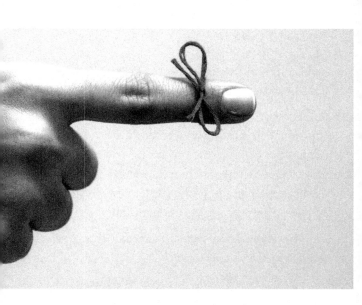

INTRODUCTION

George Washington Carver stands alongside Thomas Edison as one of the greatest inventors who has ever lived.

Carver's accomplishments are indeed astounding—and made even more so by the fact that he was a black man, living during a time when the doors of education and equal opportunity were not open to blacks in the United States.

Carver was a humble man, a man of faith who spent much time in prayer every day. And he was fond of explaining his success by saying that he had asked God to reveal to him the secrets of the universe. And instead, God, in His wisdom, had responded by showing him the secrets of the peanut.

But how great were the secrets that were contained in that little peanut!

With God's help, George Washington Carver took that seemingly insignificant little plant, and used it to create more than thirty important inventions.

It's amazing how many of God's benefits were packed into the lowly little peanut. But, you see, that's the way our God is. He has loaded up His creation with ways to benefit us.

It's interesting, isn't it, that some people can go through life without stopping to think about any of God's benefits? Turn their attention to the beauty of the sky on a starry night, and they're not impressed. Take them to the Grand Canyon and show them the glory and grandeur of that piece of God's handiwork, and they're likely to yawn in your face.

But a man of vision and faith—a man like George Washington Carver—can pick up a peanut, and have the vision, wisdom and understanding to see the many benefits of God that are locked inside that little shell.

Some people will tell you that they've never seen a miracle, when miracles are happening all around them every day.

Jesus Christ had harsh words for the people who lived in the cities of Chorazin and Bethsaida, telling them that if the mighty works that had been done in those cities had been done in Tyre and Sidon, the people of those towns would have repented and, therefore, would have been spared the destruction which befell them. How sad it will be when judgment day comes for those who have lived their entire lives blinded to the glory and majesty of God—who simply refuse to see.

My purpose in writing this book is to help you understand the benefits of God—the miracles that exist all around you. God's benefits are built into the life of every believer, if only you will accept them. He wants to give you His benefits, but before He can do that, your hands must be open and ready to receive them, just as George Washington Carver's mind was open and ready to receive the benefits that existed in that little peanut.

The miracles and mighty acts that God has performed in the past make up the history that we Christians cherish today. How thrilling it is to read about the great things God has done through the prophets, the apostles, and, of course, through the hands of His own Son. Those stories from the Bible should serve to encourage and strengthen us. And yet we are totally wrong if we think that the miracles of God are relegated to the past.

God is still in the miracle-working business today, and the mighty acts He is doing in our time will make up the history of tomorrow. If the Lord tarries, we will have an opportunity to convey in detail to our grandchildren what God has done in our generation. But we will be able to do this only if we pay attention to all of the good things God is doing among us today. In other words, only if we remember all His benefits can we pass this wonderful knowledge on down to generations that are yet to be born—if the world lasts that long.

> *Therefore, it is necessary that we with more diligence keep the things which we have heard, so that we do not fall.*   (Hebrews 2:1)

That verse says that we ought to give the more earnest heed to the things that we have heard, lest at any time we should let them slip. Our generation has seen many mighty miracles of God, and we cannot let them slip away from us. We must remember them, hold onto them, and tell our children about them with joy and thanksgiving. We cannot take for granted the fresh anointing that God is giving us. If you remember, cherish, and tell others about the benefits that God has brought your way, you will be blessed all the more—and so will those with whom you come into contact.

> *Bless the LORD, O my soul, and all that is within me, bless the name of his holiness. Bless the LORD, O my soul, and forget not all his benefits: who forgives all thine iniquities; who heals all thy diseases; who redeems thy life from destruction; who crowns thee with mercy and compassion; who satisfies thy mouth with good things so that thy youth is renewed like the eagle's. The LORD executes righteousness and justice unto all that suffer violence.* (Psalm 103:1–6)

1

BLESS THE LORD

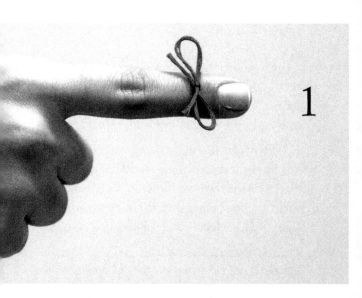

BLESS THE LORD

Recently, as I was praying and preparing for a meeting, the Holy Spirit brought to my mind the words of Psalm 103:1–2:

> O my soul, and all that is within me, bless the
> name of his holiness...O my soul, and forget
> not all his benefits.

The words *"forget not all his benefits"* kept coming to me. I suddenly realized that when we forget His benefits we allow despair, hopelessness, and depression to find a dwelling in our souls—in our minds.

I believe this is one of the reasons that mental illness is on the increase in the world today. People have not been taught how to bless the Lord, and so they are held captive by negative thinking and doubt, and despair and hopelessness are able to overtake them.

People have not been taught how to bless the Lord, and so they are held captive by negative thinking and doubt, and despair and hopelessness are able to overtake them.

That's exactly what happened to the first king of Israel: Saul.

If anyone had a reason to be thankful for what the Lord had done for him, it was Saul. Of all the people of Israel, Saul had been chosen by God to be king. What a terrific honor!

Of course, at the time, he was a humble, godly young man who was so lacking in pride that he tried to hide so that Samuel couldn't anoint him as king. But Saul went on to be a strong leader. God gave him great riches and power. He led the Israelites into victory after victory over their enemies. But somewhere along the way, he forgot all about God's benefits. He fell into deep depression. He became subject to terrible mood swings. And he descended into disobedience.

At the same time, a young boy named David was continually doing his best to bless God—even though his life wasn't nearly as exciting or glamorous as Saul's was. Saul was the king, while David was a shepherd. Saul lived in luxurious splendor, while David lived a simple life. Saul was a great and mighty warrior, whereas David was the youngest and least in his family—ridiculed and looked down upon by all of his older brothers.

And yet David never ceased blessing God with his hymns and spiritual songs. He meditated day and night on the benefits of His Lord.

And, of course, we all know what happened. The kingdom was taken away from Saul and given to David.

Now David wasn't perfect. He committed adultery with Bathsheba. He schemed to have her husband killed in battle. Some of his children were rebellious and wicked. But through everything that happened to him, he never forgot the many ways in which God had blessed him. He thought about those things, and he blessed the Lord because of them.

Now I don't know about you, but it sounds a little presumptuous for me to think that I can actually bless the Lord. But I know that I can, because the Bible tells me I can. It not only tells me that I can, but commands me to do it.

Isn't it good to know that you have the ability to bring joy to the heart of the Creator of the universe? We all need to learn how to praise and bless the Lord, because of what He has done for us, and because of Who He is.

I encourage you to train your mind to bless the Lord in all situations, remembering that the way you think will determine, to a great extent, what your future is going to be like. The mind is the battleground of the spirit. It is also the place where your thinking and behavior patterns are established, and where you store your knowledge of who God is as well as the remembrance of His goodness.

The mind is the battleground of the spirit.

It's vitally important that we learn to bless the Lord, at *all* times, including those occasions when we don't feel much like blessing Him.

Do you have a headache? Bless the Lord anyway, remembering that healing comes from His hand.

Your boss is on your back? That's the perfect time to bless the Lord—because He understands what you are going through and will give you the strength and wisdom to deal with the situation.

You feel that your friends have turned against you? Bless the Lord, because He is a friend who will never desert you.

God wants us to act on His Word. When His Word says, "Bless the Lord, O my soul," that's what He wants us to do, even in the most difficult of situations. It is imperative that we learn to be led by God, and not by our feelings.

Think about what Christ would have done if He had decided to let His feelings dictate His behavior. Do you think He would have gone to the cross to die for us? Of course not. He did what He knew He had to do instead of what He wanted to do.

If we are led by our feelings, our spiritual condition is not fit to fulfill the plan that God has for us. One day, our feelings may tell us to praise God, and the next day, they may tell us to be angry with Him because He hasn't answered our prayers in the exact way we wanted Him to. Some people are like that. You might call them spiritual yo-yos, and it's no wonder that they never do anything great for the kingdom of God. Always remember that your feelings are fickle. They change from day to day, but that doesn't mean that God has changed. He is always the same, and your trust must come from knowing who God is and having an understanding that His Word will endure forever. As it says in Matthew 24:35, "*Heaven and earth shall pass away, but my words shall not pass away.*"

A few years ago, there was a very popular philosophy that can be expressed in a very few words: "If it feels good, do it."

It sounds pretty good, doesn't it? After all, we all like to feel good, and nobody likes to feel bad, so why not just do the easy and comfortable thing all the time?

But you know what? A whole bunch of people who tried living by that philosophy found out that it just didn't work. It didn't work because sometimes the things that felt the best were the worst for you.

People felt like taking drugs because drugs made them feel good. But in the end, they wound up addicted or dead from overdoses.

They engaged in promiscuous sex, because that, too, made them feel good, but in the end, they wound up with terrible sexually transmitted diseases and with emotional problems, and they soon discovered that there really is no such thing as "casual" sex.

They "dropped out," and took life easy because that felt good, only to find that this was a lifestyle that led to hunger and homelessness.

They refused to listen to authority of any type, because that *didn't* feel good, but, as a result, they found themselves drifting into lives of chaos and aimlessness.

If we were all to live by the way we feel and through the discernment of our natural intellect, some of us would be very far away from the Lord.

No, you cannot be led by your feelings. As an entire generation discovered, they just may lead you down the road to destruction.

Oftentimes, a person's feelings are going to be in direct opposition to the Word of God. That's because we live in a sinful, fallen world, and we are prone to sinful, fallen impulses and habits. If we were all to live by the way we feel and through the discernment of our natural intellect, some of us would be very far away from the Lord.

The first time a person's mind comes in contact with the demonstration of the power of God, there is a battle between the religious ideas, those that are not based on biblical principles, and spiritual truths that come from God. It is at this time that the human intellect tries to analyze and dissect everything. If a solid foundation has not been built upon the truths contained within the Word of God, the mind will rule against the things of God.

In other words, unless it is properly trained and grounded in God's truth, the human mind can be a very earthly, fleshy thing—believing only what it can see or feel. God says one thing, but the human mind says, *Well, that just doesn't sound right to me. I think I'll do it* **this** *way.*

Gideon

God told him that the army he had put together was too large and that he should let anyone who felt afraid to go home. And then, even after all of those men left, God said that the army was *still* too large, so He came up with a plan whereby the vast majority of the rest of the men would also be sent home.

And then, after all of that, God told Gideon and his men to fight with clay jars and trumpets instead of with weapons.

If Gideon had been listening to his human understanding, he would have been saying, "I can't believe God thinks this army is too big. If anything it's too small! I've got to find some more men."

But Gideon didn't follow his feelings. He followed the Word of God, and gained a mighty victory over the Midianites.

Joshua

And what about Joshua and the wall of Jericho? Did it make sense for the Israelites to march around that wall and blow their trumpets? Not to the human intellect, it didn't. But that was what God said to do and it worked.

Naaman

One more example? Naaman was the Syrian general who was healed of leprosy by the prophet Elisha. He was offended when Elisha told him to wash himself in the River Jordan. He almost refused to do it. But then, at the last moment, after being talked into it by his servant, he did as the prophet had suggested, thus obeying God's command—and he was healed!

I am often amazed by the fact that sinners seem to have more common sense that many Christians do. When a sinner is in any type of need, he seeks the advice of an expert—a person who, by the standards of the world, has the knowledge and experience necessary to help him. And whatever advice the expert gives is usually followed without question. There is a feeling that, "Well, this guy's an expert. He knows what he's talking about, so I had better do what he says."

But, you know, there is no greater authority than God. It doesn't matter what the subject is, He knows more about it than anyone else could possibly know. It makes sense then, doesn't it, that when God tells us to do something, we ought to listen very carefully.

Now one of the most important ways He speaks to us is through His Word—the Bible. The point I'm making is that we should never question the instructions God gives us through His Holy Book, because they are indisputably true and totally for our benefit. Have you seen the bumper sticker that reads: "God said it, I believe it, and that settles it"? That's the way it ought to be for us. If God said it, then we believe it to be true, and the matter is closed to further discussion.

First John 5:3 tells us, *"For this is the love of God, that we keep his commandments: and his commandments are not grievous."* God's commandments are not burdensome, and that's true. God didn't think up a bunch of laws just to keep us all bound up, or because He wanted to keep us from having a good time. No, He gave us laws and precepts that are for *our benefit.*

When we carefully follow the laws that have been built into this universe, we will flourish and prosper. When we try to live in disobedience to what God says, we are going to get ourselves into big trouble.

When we try to live in disobedience
to what God says, we are going to get
ourselves into big trouble.

Think about some of the natural laws that God has built into His creation. For example, consider the law of gravity. Suppose a friend said, "You know, I really think the law of gravity is ridiculous. I don't see any reason why I ought to live my life in obedience to something like that. It really stifles me."

You'd think your friend had lost more than a little bit of his mind. But then you'd probably ask him to explain to you exactly what he was talking about.

"Well, I really want to fly, and I don't see any reason why I shouldn't fly. So I'm just going to take an elevator up to the top of the Empire State Building and I'm going to jump off and fly all around New York City."

Of course, if your friend was serious, and if he really tried to do something like that, you know what would happen. His flight would be a short and fast one—straight down. That's because your friend's actions would be governed by the law of gravity, no matter how much he did or did not believe in it!

What's more, the law of gravity was built into this universe for our benefit and not for our harm. If it wasn't for gravity, we all would float off into space. The planets wouldn't revolve around the sun the way they have to in order to sustain life. The air we breathe would quickly disappear.

So you see, gravity is one of those laws that keeps us alive. It exists for our benefit. But if you try to rebel against it and go jumping off of a tall building or into the Grand Canyon, you will be the one who winds up broken, not the law.

All of God's laws are like that, whether we are talking about natural laws or spiritual laws.

For example, God tells us not to murder or steal or commit adultery. Can you imagine what a society would be like in which people thought it was fine to do those things? There would be no order, no peace, and life would be hellish. Obedience to these laws of God, then, is the cornerstone upon which civilized society is built.

It is so important to "*forget not his benefits.*" And one of the very important benefits God gives us is His holy Word. Without it, mankind would be floundering around in the darkness. But God's Word is like a beacon, shining in the darkness, guiding us safely through whatever storms may come along.

It's also important to remember that one of the ways we can bless God is to live in obedience to His Word. This brings a happiness and joy to God's heart. As Samuel told Saul after Saul had disobeyed God's direct command: "*To obey is better than sacrifice, and to harken than the fat of rams*" (1 Samuel 15:22).

It is also true, of course, that God speaks to individual Christians today, giving us specific words of wisdom and guidance. If you are in tune with God's Holy Spirit, spending as much time as possible in prayer and meditation, then certainly He is going to reveal His specific will for your life.

Now there are some people who have been fooled—who thought they were listening to the voice of God when they were really being distracted by the enemy. But that will not happen if you are living a life of godly obedience. It will not happen if you are totally yielded to the Holy Spirit and have set aside your own fleshly desires. It will not happen if you are spending quality time in the Word of God, letting it sink deep down into your soul. And it will not happen if you are actively involved in a faithful, Bible-believing church, where you have the counsel of godly, spiritually mature men and women.

As a Christian, you should never question anything God asks you to do. If you are certain the Lord is asking you to do something, then run and do it without questioning Him. Some people aren't profiting in every area of their lives because they aren't willing to obey God at the time He talks to them. They feel that in six months they might be ready to do whatever it is that God is telling them to do—but not right now. Unfortunately, six months later, it could be that the opportunity God had lain before you has passed. Because you wouldn't do the thing He wanted you to do, He gave the job to someone else. Because you wouldn't receive the blessing He was trying to put into your hands, He gave it to someone else.

Jesus said that no one who puts his hand to the plow and looks back is fit for the kingdom of God. (See Luke 9:62.) In other words, when God calls you to something, your job is to run as fast as you can to do it. We bless the Lord when we show Him that we are totally committed to doing His will. We sadden Him when we show by our actions that we don't really believe He has our best interests at heart—when we show that we have forgotten His benefits.

When God calls you to something,
your job is to run as fast as you can to do it.
We bless the Lord when we show Him that we
are totally committed to doing His will.

Before moving on, I want to direct your attention back to the first verse of Psalm 103 for just a moment. Specifically, I want to look at the phrase *"all that is within me."* What does it mean for *"all that is within me"* to bless the holy name of the Lord? It means that God wants us to bless Him in every way we can: spiritually, mentally and physically—and that includes singing, dancing, and the lifting up of holy hands through a pure heart. When your entire being is harmoniously blessing God, you will start remembering all of His benefits!

DISCUSSION QUESTIONS:

1. What are some of the ways in which you can train your mind to bless the Lord in all situations?

2. What is the difference between being led by our feelings and being led by the Spirit?

3. How have you experienced God's laws as being for your benefit?

4. Have you ever ignored God when He told you to do something? What happened?

2

FORGETTING
THE PAST

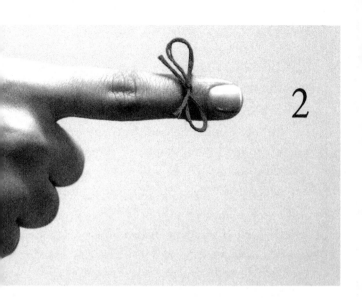

FORGETTING THE PAST

She sat there, holding her face in her hands. When she finally looked up, huge tears were making their way down her cheeks.

"I just can't!" she sobbed. "I just can't forget about it."

"Jane," I said, firmly. "It's over and done. It has been washed away by the blood of Jesus. He has forgiven you, so don't you think it's time you forgave yourself?"

"If only I could believe that," she continued to weep. "If only I could know for sure that God has *really* forgiven me."

What had Jane done that was so wrong? She had become involved in a brief extra-marital affair. It hadn't lasted very long. It had been over for years. She had long ago confessed it to God and asked His forgiveness. And, of course, He was willing to forgive and forget her sin the moment she had repented and asked Him to. But she couldn't accept it.

She was holding onto the past as tight as she possibly could, and would not let it go.

Had Jane done wrong? Yes, of course she had. Was her sin something that grieved the heart of God? Again, the answer is yes, of course. It wasn't any "minor" thing. There are no sins that are minor. All sin is horrible because it serves to separate us from God. But there is no sin—with the exception of blasphemy against the Holy Spirit—that is so great that it cannot be washed away by Christ's cleansing blood.

Jane was in bondage when God wanted her to be free—in fact, had paid the price for her to be free.

And because she was held captive by the sins of her past, she was not living the life God wanted her to live today, nor was she able to freely bless the Lord.

All sin is horrible because it serves to separate us from God. But there is no sin—with the exception of blasphemy against the Holy Spirit— that is so great that it cannot be washed away by Christ's cleansing blood.

Thankfully, she has come to the place where she now understands the war that was going on in her soul. God wanted her to be free, but Satan kept pointing to those old sins of the past and saying, "Just look at what you did! You are a really terrible person! How could you think God would forgive you for this?"

You see, for your soul to freely bless the Lord, you must forget about your past—and move on into the future. Satan will try to control you, just the way he tried to control Jane, by bringing up past shortcomings and mistakes over and over again. It will help to remember the biblical truth that *all have sinned, and come short of the glory of God; being justified freely by his grace through the redemption that is in Christ Jesus* (Romans 3:23–24).

Everyone has sinned. There's not a person on this planet who hasn't fallen short of God's perfect will. But God is faithful and desires to forgive us of our unrighteousness—and when God forgives, He also forgets. He wants us to follow His example and stop dwelling on those actions of the past that have already been forgiven. Don't allow your soul to remember those things that are now under the blood of Christ. Don't allow them to dominate your present and affect your future.

God is faithful and desires to
forgive us of our unrighteousness—and when
God forgives, He also forgets.

We need to follow these words of the apostle Paul, as recorded in Philippians 3:13–14:

> *Brethren, I count not myself to have apprehended: but this one thing I do, forgetting those things which are behind, and reaching forth unto those things which are before, I press toward the mark for the prize of the high calling of God in Christ Jesus.*

If anyone had reason to be bound by his past, it was the apostle Paul. After all, he had been responsible for out-and-out persecution of the Lord's people. He had been there when Stephen was stoned to death, watching the coats of the men who killed him. (See Acts 7.)

Acts 8:3 says that, "*As for Saul* [his name was later changed to Paul], *he made havoc of the church, entering every house, and dragging off men and women, committing them to prison*" (NKJV).

Imagine how he must have felt when Jesus Christ appeared to him on the road to Damascus—when he discovered that the people he had been persecuting were God's children! How terrible it must have been to know that he had been fighting so furiously against God's kingdom and God's people.

But Paul didn't dwell on the past. Instead, he concentrated on the task at hand and the future that lay before him. How very much we can learn from the actions of a man like Paul!

Let me tell you about someone else who never would have discovered all of God's benefits if he had been bound by the past. His name was Peter, and he was one of the original twelve apostles.

He was impetuous, impulsive, and not exactly a tower of strength in his early days.

For example, when he saw Jesus walking on the water, he wanted to do the same thing. Jesus said, "Come." But the apostle hadn't taken more than a few steps out onto the Sea of Galilee when fear overcame him, and he began to sink like a stone statue. Imagine how embarrassed he must have felt when the Lord had to rescue him, and he had to sit there in the boat— soaking wet and shivering in the cold, while the other apostles did their best to stifle their laughter.

Next, the scene shifts to the garden of Gethsemane, where impetuous Peter tries to fight off an entire legion of Roman soldiers all by himself, and winds up cutting off the high priest's servant's ear. Even at that late date, even after all of the times Christ had tried to explain to His apostles that His death was necessary. Peter still didn't understand.

And finally, the saddest scene of them all, Peter standing outside the high priest's house while Jesus is on trial inside. You know the story. It goes something like this.

One of the high priest's servant girls thinks she recognizes him.

"I know that man. He was with Jesus."

"Who me?" Peter replies. "No, I've never met the man."

The girl is persistent, and starts to tell the others gathered there, "I'm sure that he's one of them."

This time Peter acts indignant.

"I'm sure I don't know what you're talking about!"

Peter is not out of the woods yet, because the people still don't believe him.

"But you must have been with him," someone says. "After all, your speech gives you away. You have a Galilean accent."

This time Peter explodes into a rage. "I told you I don't know the man!" And he punctuates his denial with cursing and swearing. And, of course, you know what happened next. Peter immediately heard the crowing of the rooster, and he remembered the words Jesus had spoken just a few hours earlier: *"Before the rooster crows twice, you will deny Me three times"* (Mark 14:72 NKJV).

And what had Peter said in response to these words from the Lord: "If I have to die with You, I will not deny You!"

How empty and hollow those words must have sounded to him now. How could he have let his Lord down like that? At that very moment, I'm sure Peter wanted to disappear right into the earth.

But, like his contemporary Paul, Peter did not let the past hold him back. Instead, he went on to be one of the greatest of all the apostles. It was Peter who boldly preached the first gospel sermon on the Day of Pentecost. It was Peter who stood boldly before government officials who had the power to take his life and declared that he would not stop talking about Jesus no matter what they did to him. (See Acts 4:19–22.) It was Peter who ultimately met the same fate as His Lord, but who, according to tradition, demanded that he be crucified upside down because he did not consider himself worthy to die in the same way Jesus died. In other words, from his shaky beginnings, Peter went on to be a great leader of courage and power—*not even flinching* in the face of death.

Suppose those great men of faith had been held hostage by the failures of their past?

From his shaky beginnings, Peter went on to be a great leader of courage and power— *not even flinching* in the face of death.

Let me give you a couple of other examples from modern times. Did you know that Thomas Edison tried and failed nearly one thousand times in his efforts to invent the incandescent light bulb? Talk about failure! And yet, he counted every failed experiment as the elimination of a wrong way of doing things meaning that he was always one step closer to the *right* way of doing things.

As another example, consider Winston Churchill, the man who provided such inspirational leadership for Great Britain and, really, for much of the rest of the free world during World War II and beyond. Because of certain "tactical blunders" made by young Captain Winston Churchill during the fighting in World War I, he was considered "washed up," his career in military and public service over. If Churchill had been content to sit and brood over the failures of his past, chances are very good that you and I never would have heard of him. He would have been nothing more than another obscure name from the distant past.

But like Paul and Peter and Thomas Edison, Churchill learned from his failures. He let those failures propel him forward into a successful future instead of chaining him to the past.

In the entire history of the world, there has only been one person who did not commit a single sin, and that person is Jesus Christ, the Son of the living God.

What is more, the only people who never fail are people who never try to do anything! Remember that when you're tempted to get down on yourself. You have sinned? Certainly. You are a human being, and *all* human beings have sinned. You have failed? That is an indication, at least, that you were willing to try.

I'm sure you've heard it said, "It is no disgrace to fall, but it is a disgrace to lie there." Well, that's true. But what is even more important to remember is that because of Jesus Christ, nobody has to just lie there. The Lord is there, with His hand outstretched to you, ready and willing to pick you up and get you started on the right path again. He wants to help you!

Dwelling on the problems and failures of your past can be a heavy weight that pulls you down. You may be trying to soar with the eagles, but you'll feel instead like you're crawling with the tortoises—and trying to crawl through quicksand at that!

Furthermore, if you don't permit God to free your soul from the heavy weight that comes about from dwelling in the past, you will not be able to hear the Spirit of God.

That's because your mind will become contaminated by wrong thoughts, feelings and imaginations that will hinder your walk with God.

God doesn't want you to dwell in the past.

Satan *does* want you to dwell in the past. Specifically, the devil loves to keep reminding you of the wrong acts you have done. The Bible says that Satan is the accuser of the brethren (see Revelation 12:10)—but there is no reason in the world why any born-again Christian has to listen to him.

Once you have made a decision to align your thoughts with the Word of God, it is imperative that you invest as much time as possible putting His Word in your mind.

Instead, every Christian needs to be in tune with the Words that come from the mouth and mind of God. Saturate yourself in the Scriptures. Let them seep down into your soul where they really become a part of your makeup.

There is life in the Word of God, and He has given it to us for our benefit.

Once you have made a decision to align your thoughts with the Word of God, it is imperative that you invest as much time as possible putting His Word in your mind. In my own experience, I have devoted years to investing in the things of God. And I cannot tell you how often I feel glad about that. I am continuously reaping profits from that investment in all areas of my life—and more and more I am made to realize that unless a person's body, mind, and spirit are involved with the things of God, that person cannot live a life of complete victory.

Please, read the instructions. God gave them to us for our benefit. He expects us to read them!

It's hard for me to understand why any Christian would not want to spend time in the Bible. I've heard the Bible referred to as "the Manufacturer's handbook," and I think that's a pretty good description. God is the manufacturer, not only of this universe we live in, but of you and me and every other human being. And after He created everything we see including us — He gave us His instruction book, in the form of the Bible. If you want to know about the way things are, then you need to read the Bible. If you want to know what you can do to make life better for yourself and the people you love, then you ought to read the Bible.

Have you ever tried to put together a bicycle or something else equally as complicated on Christmas Eve? If so, have you ever tried to do it *without* reading the instructions that came with it?

You know, some people are just impatient.

"I don't need that instruction booklet. Just give me a couple of wrenches, a screwdriver and a hammer and I'll have that bike together in no time!"

Four hours later, that person is usually still hard at work on something that doesn't even remotely begin to resemble a bicycle! He's starting to panic, because this thing has to be waiting under the tree on Christmas morning, and it has to look like a bicycle by then—so finally he says, "Oh, all right...let me read those instructions." And he has to go dig them out of the trash.

Or maybe he's got the bicycle together, but he's got 437 screws and a couple of bolts left over. "Well," he says, scratching his head, "I don't know where all these extra parts came from...but I think it *looks* okay."

Of course, chances are that the first or second time that bike is used, it's going to fall apart.

If you don't read the instructions, you can get yourself into a lot of trouble, even if you're only talking about bicycles! When it comes to living life on this planet of ours, failure to read the instructions can be downright deadly!

Please, read the instructions. God gave them to us for our benefit. He expects us to read them!

I have also heard the Bible referred to as a love letter from God. I think that's another good description.

Now I don't think most people who get love letters let them lie around collecting dust for weeks or even years before they read them.

"Hey, Joe, aren't you going to read this letter."

"Nah...I'll probably read it tomorrow — or the next day."

"But, Joe...it looks like it's a letter from Rita. Aren't you supposed to be in love with her."

"Oh," Joe says, "I am...I am...! It's just that...well, I'm kind of busy right now, so I'll just try to read it when I get the time."

What would you think of someone who acted like that. I'm pretty sure you'd think that he wasn't as much in love with the girl as he pretended to be.

That's just not how lovers act. If Joe loved Rita, he would read her letter as soon as he got it. And he'd probably read it again—and again and again—until he had practically memorized it. *That's* how lovers act.

Do you love God? Then read the love letter He has written to you in the form of the Bible.

It is there for your benefit, for your instruction, for your edification.

Remember these words that the apostle Paul wrote to his son in the faith, Timothy:

All Scripture is given by inspiration of God, and is profitable for doctrine, for reproof, for correction, for instruction in righteousness, that the man of God may be complete, thoroughly equipped for every good work.

(2 Timothy 3:16)

Next, we'll discuss in detail more of the exciting benefits God has made available for *all* of his children!

DISCUSSION QUESTIONS:

1. Why is it so hard to let go of things in the past and give them to God?

2. Why is to your benefit to let go of things in the past and give them to God?

3. What are some of the ways that Satan uses to make you dwell on the past?

4. How to you defeat Satan when he continually brings up your past?

3

FORGET NOT ALL
HIS BENEFITS

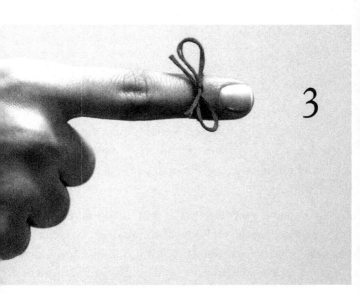

FORGET NOT ALL
HIS BENEFITS

Are you a child of the king? You are if you have surrendered your life to God's control—if you have accepted Jesus Christ as your Lord and Savior, if you have the Holy Spirit living within you.

And as a child of the king, you have been given a number of tremendous benefits.

If you've ever been to London, I'm sure you've been to Buckingham Palace. What a magnificent place it is! And it's only one of the many beautiful palaces and estates that are maintained for the British royal family.

Being a member of the royal family surely has its benefits! And, you know, if you have been reconciled to God through the shed blood of Jesus Christ, then *you* are a member of the royal family—and I mean *the* royal family. The head of this family is not a king or the queen mother, but God Himself.

Psalm 103:3–6 lists some of the benefits that belong to anyone who is a member of God's family. This passage of Scripture tells us that for this person, it is God:

> *Who forgiveth all thy iniquities; who healeth all thy diseases; who redeemeth thy life from destruction; who crowneth thee with loving kindness and tender mercies; who satisfieth thy mouth with good things; so that thy youth is renewed like the eagle's. The LORD executeth righteousness and judgment for all that are oppressed.*

Every child of God who has repented of his sins, believes that Jesus is the Son of God and has accepted Him as Savior, has received salvation. With salvation comes many earthly benefits that we will not need in heaven, but that will certainly help us to live a victorious, fulfilled life here on earth. As we look at each of the blessings listed in this Psalm, we see God's abundant grace and provisions, which are enough to cover all of our needs.

Let's take a closer look at these benefits:

With salvation comes many earthly
benefits that we will not need in heaven,
but that will certainly help us to live a victorious,
fulfilled life here on earth.

---

1) GOD FORGIVES ALL OUR INIQUITIES

If you are a born-again Christian who is filled with the Holy Spirit, and if you are living in pursuit of holiness, you can enjoy the benefit of knowing that your weaknesses and sins can be forgiven and removed from God's record.

The Bible makes it very clear that God's forgiving grace is available to all. You don't have to beg and plead to get Him to forgive you. You don't have to perform some great act to prove that you're worthy of being forgiven. You don't have to punish yourself.

All you have to do is ask, sincerely, and God agrees to wipe the slate clean. He applies the blood and righteousness of His Son to your life, and you are able to stand justified before Him. Perhaps you've heard it said that a good definition of the word *justified* is "just-as-if-I'd-never-sinned." I like that. I like it because that's the way it is as far as God is concerned. He's not going to hold it over you the next time you make a mistake and say, "Hey, didn't I just forgive you for this a couple of months ago? It's not going to be so easy for me to forgive you this time!"

No...because when He forgives He forgets. As far as He's concerned, that last sin never happened at all.

I think this is important to know, because some people have particular sins that get a grip on them—and sometimes these people give up because they think they've let God down.

For example, consider someone who is an alcoholic, who is struggling to overcome his tendency to drink. He knows drinking is wrong, and he wants to stop, but he's struggling with it. Now don't get me wrong.

The Bible makes it very clear that
God's forgiving grace is available to all. You don't
have to beg and plead to get Him to forgive you.

Certainly I believe that God can deliver people instantly from any addiction, including alcohol. I've seen it happen instantaneously many times, and I praise God when it does. On the other hand, I have seen instances where, for whatever reason, there wasn't instantaneous deliverance.

And so, this person gets drunk...feels terrible about it, and asks for God's forgiveness, vowing to God and himself that it won't happen again.

Only it does happen again...and again...and again. Eventually, this person thinks, "I can't keep asking God for forgiveness of the same old thing." He may even turn his back on God, feeling that He's let the Lord down and that forgiveness is no longer available.

Well, it just isn't so. I don't care if it's the 100th time you've asked His forgiveness for the same sin. If you have asked sincerely, and if you are really trying to live for Him, then He doesn't remember the other 99 times *at all*!

Now I want to make it clear that I'm not talking about the person who is a willful sinner. It is not possible to think, "Well, I can go ahead and indulge myself in this sin, because God will forgive me anyway." That's not the way it works. There is no forgiveness without sincere repentance, but there is *always* forgiveness *with* sincere repentance.

I also hasten to add that anyone who is truly living for Jesus should see his life transformed, as he begins to more and more take on the likeness of Christ. God will not only forgive you of your sins, but He will help you gain victory over them.

My point is not that it is all right to be held in the grip of sin—but rather that God's mercy and grace is deep enough to cover anything you may have done, or anything you may be involved in right now.

Remember that the Psalm says that God forgives *all* your iniquities. That's an important point, because the devil is always trying to make people believe that *all* doesn't really mean *all*. But when God says "all," He means everything—not just one small action or one major event. God forgives and forgets it *all*.

As 1 John 1:9 says, *"If we confess our sins, he is faithful and just to forgive us our sins, and to cleanse us from all unrighteousness."*

It doesn't make a bit of difference what you have done publicly or privately—God will forgive you if you come to Him with a sincere heart.

There's that word again: *All* unrighteousness.

I often talk to people who are being held back in their Christian walk because of the guilt they harbor over secret sins. Sometimes they feel like phonies, because they know things about themselves that nobody else knows.

"Oh, pastor, you don't know what I've done...."

No, I don't. But God does. And it doesn't matter. He's willing to forgive you anyway, and to cleanse you from all unrighteousness, and that's what's important. It doesn't make a bit of difference what you have done publicly or privately—God will forgive you if you come to Him with a sincere heart and pray a prayer like this one: "Father, Son and Holy Spirit, I have sinned against You and Your Word. I ask for forgiveness today. I am sorry for what I have done."

If you have been saved for any length of time but still feel the guilt of your past sins, you need to be aware that this bondage comes from an evil spirit that is trying to dominate you and hold you back—and thus stop you from doing what God has called you to do. If that is the case with you, you need to get hold of the spiritual weapons that God has provided. In His Name and with His Word, you must claim the blood of Jesus and cast guilt and condemnation out of your life.

Romans 8:1–2 tells us that,

> *There is therefore now no condemnation to them which are in Christ Jesus, who walk not after the flesh but after the Spirit. For the law of the Spirit of life in Christ Jesus bath made me free from the law of sin and death.*

Did you hear that? If you belong to Jesus you are free from condemnation. That is a great verse to turn to when you need comfort and reassurance.

I know a man who says he had a great deal of difficulty getting set free from his past sins. He had given his life to Christ, but he just couldn't feel that he had been forgiven of all the things he'd done. And so, every night, after his wife was asleep, he'd slip out of bed, go in the bathroom, close the door, and get down on his knees and beg for forgiveness.

This went on for a couple of weeks until, one night, on his knees in the bathroom, he heard the small, still voice of God. And it said, "Why do you keep asking Me to forgive you when I did it the first time you asked me?"

There was no condemnation in the voice. Only a gentle reminder that forgiveness had already been obtained, that "you don't have to worry about those things anymore."

And that's the way it is with God. He forgives and He forgets.

Now let's take a look at the second benefit listed in Psalm 103.

2) GOD HEALS ALL OUR DISEASES

God provides healing for all types of diseases, whether we are talking about illnesses of the body or the mind. The Gospels are filled with instances in which Jesus "healed them all," "delivered them all," and declared "that all" should be saved. Don't ever let Satan deceive you by telling you that the promise of healing doesn't include you. It includes everybody!

I suggest that you study the Scriptures on healing until they have become real to you until faith has risen up in you. You are a child of God and, therefore, you are entitled to healing. It is one of God's benefits for His children.

Isaiah 53:6 tells us that we are healed by the stripes on Christ's body. In other words, the blood of Christ provides for salvation, and it also provides for our healing. When Christ was whipped prior to His crucifixion, the beating left bloody "stripes" all over His back. It is through those stripes that we are healed. In other words, Jesus paid the price so that we might be forgiven of our sins, *and* so that we might be healed of our diseases.

A man named Henry had a brain tumor. He underwent a seven-hour operation, after which doctors told him they were sorry, but they were unable to entirely remove the malignancy. It was only a matter of time before it grew back to its full size, and eventually it would take his life. There simply wasn't anything further they could do for him.

But Henry copied Isaiah 53 and taped it to his bathroom mirror. Every morning, as he was shaving and getting ready to face the day, he read those words and reminded himself that his healing had been provided by those stripes on Christ's back.

Henry didn't feel well. He was nauseated. He had terrible headaches. He was weak.

When Christ was whipped prior to His crucifixion, the beating left bloody "stripes" all over His back. It is through those stripes that we are healed.

And he says, "I didn't lie to myself about how I was feeling. I was feeling terrible. But I kept reading that verse, and kept on believing that the healing in the atonement was available to me and that day by day I was getting better."

And you know what? He did get better.

Henry's brain tumor operation was more than fourteen years ago. And today he's strong and healthy, without any sign of illness. He has been completely healed.

That's only one case. I know of literally hundreds of others—people who were healed by the grace of God, even though their doctors had told them there wasn't any hope. God healed all of these people, and He is willing and ready to heal you, too. Your healing may come in an instant—or it may come, like Henry's did, over time. But believe, and hold on to God, and it will come.

Sickness is not from God. It comes from the devil. But, Christ has power over the devil, and His power is available to you.

In Matthew 8:16, we read,

> *When the even was come, they brought unto him many that were possessed with devils: and he cast out the spirits with his word, and healed **all** that were sick.*

Notice that word again: *all.*

In Luke 13:10–17, there is an account of Jesus healing a bent and crippled woman on the Sabbath day. After healing the woman, Jesus ascribed her illness directly to the devil, saying that Satan had held her bound for eighteen years. We can see from this that illness often has to do with Satan and his evil intentions. As for God, He tells us:

> *For I know the thoughts that I think toward you, says the LORD, thoughts of peace and not of evil, to give you a future and a hope.*
>
> (Jeremiah 29:11)

God's desire for you is that you be well and at peace in body, mind and spirit. He does not want you bound up by sickness.

James 4:7 tells us that if we resist the devil he will flee from us. So allow the Holy Spirit within you to be so strong that you are able to do just that—resist him. Don't ever forget the power that you have over Satan. And, what's more, don't ever believe one of Satan's favorite lies, which is: "God is testing you through this illness."

God wants the very best for you, and that most definitely does *not* include illness.

> *Every good gift and every perfect gift is from above, and cometh down from the Father of lights, with whom is no variableness, neither shadow of turning.* (James 1:17)

God's greatest test is not to make you sick, but to see how you will react when you have obtained His benefits. Will you still tithe once you have become a wealthy man? Will you still attend church once you have been healed? Will you still preach in a small church once you have been blessed with a large ministry? How faithful are you to your commitments? God is interested in seeing how you conduct yourself and how you hold His goodness.

Through His Holy Word, God tells us that He wants to heal all our diseases. He is saying to us, "I want you to have this benefit. Don't forget my benefit of healing."

When you receive a gift at Christmas or on your birthday you don't say, "I don't want it." But that's exactly what we do with God. We try to give Him back the benefits and blessings He has designed specifically for us. He wants them to overtake us in every part of our lives.

God wants the very best for you, and that most definitely does *not* include illness.

As I write this, there's quite a bit of debate in this country about the effectiveness and necessity of President Clinton's national health-care plan. Many people are afraid of it because it's going to be so costly. But remember—God has a wonderful health-care plan for all those who belong to Him, and the only cost involved is believing in Jesus.

Now let's move on to the third benefit recorded in Psalm 103.

3) GOD REDEEMS US FROM DESTRUCTION

There are many people who, at one time or another, have experienced destruction in their lives. At times, this destruction has been a part of their family, and it has spread to every member—even from generation to generation. But God is willing and able to deliver you from such destruction. His promises not only mean freedom from generational destruction, but also from other evils that can destroy your life—alcoholism, poverty, religious control, mental illness, physical disease and relationship problems to name just a few of the ways destruction can come upon you.

In today's society it seems that I'm always hearing people talking about coming from a dysfunctional family. Dad was an alcoholic. Mom was abusive. The members of the family didn't communicate with each other. And so on.

In fact, not long ago I saw a cartoon in which a vast audience was gathered together, and the speaker was asking for all those people who came from "normal" families to raise their hands. Out of hundreds of people in the audience, there were perhaps two or three with their hands raised. That's probably a pretty accurate picture. If most people really look very closely at the families they come from, they can probably see some real problem areas.

But a Christian should never blame anything on his family background, no matter how difficult it might have been.

Perhaps you were abused in some way.

Perhaps your parents were cold and indifferent to you.

Maybe you were extremely poor.

Or your parents abused alcohol or other drugs.

Whatever happened to you doesn't have to affect you. You don't have to be tainted by it. You don't have to let it destroy you. God wants to free you from the destruction that Satan wanted to put on you through that bad family background or those bad family relationships.

I've had people say to me, "You don't understand. This is just the way my family has always been. It's my destiny!"

Nonsense.

If you are a born-again Christian, then you are a member of God's family, and your destiny is to follow in the footsteps of your Father, the King! Thanks to the power and love of Christ, you simply do not have to be affected by the bad traits of your family tree even if those traits have affected your family for generations. God wants you to be free from this type of curse so that you can provide a better heritage for your children. This is one promise of God that we must all cling to. There are bad traits and good traits in *every* family, but you can't be saved, nor can you be condemned, because of the family you come from.

God wants to free you from
the destruction that Satan wanted to put
on you through that bad family background or
those bad family relationships.

At the same time, although all of us are in the process of learning and growing, there are areas of our lives where destruction exists. One of the benefits of serving Jesus is that His power redeems us from these evils.

This benefit also means God's protection over us. You may never know how many times God has supernaturally protected you from harm that was headed your way. Perhaps He delayed you for just a moment, and that moment meant the difference between you arriving safely or getting involved in an accident. Perhaps someone meant to do you harm, but God stopped them. Perhaps you were entering into a business deal that fell apart and you didn't understand why, but it was God's hand protecting you from making a terrible mistake. You may have wanted to pursue a certain friendship or romantic relationship, but it just didn't happen the way you wanted it to. Again, this could be due to God's protection, as He kept you away from relationships and entanglements that would have been harmful to you.

> When God calls you to go and tell
> others about His saving grace,
> He will provide protection for you.

A few years ago, I read a newspaper article about an explosion that destroyed a small church in the midwest. It seems there was a gas leak, and the church went up in flames shortly after 7:30 on a Saturday night. It was a real miracle that no one was injured or killed. Why? Because the choir was supposed to arrive for rehearsal at 7:30—but for some reason, every single member of the choir was late. It wasn't a large choir—20 or 25 people, as I recall—but a series of strange "coincidences" had occurred to keep all of those people, including the choir director, from getting to the church on time.

At the time they were being delayed, I'm sure those people were annoyed. They were thinking, "This is terrible! I'm going to be late to choir practice! This makes me so angry!" But now, they can look back and see that God was working in their lives to protect them from harm. Anyone who had been on time to choir practice that night would certainly have been killed.

Keep in mind that when God calls you to go and tell others about His saving grace, He will provide protection for you. If He calls you to go into the worst, most crime-infested area of your city to preach, then do it with confidence that He will protect you. If He calls you to take the Gospel overseas to some country you'd rather not visit, you can be assured that His protection will go along with you. God will redeem you from destruction.

4) GOD CROWNS US WITH LOVING KINDNESS AND TENDER MERCIES

The Scriptures tell us that God, in His infinite love for us, has not only made provision for forgiveness of our sins, for healing of our diseases, and for deliverance from destruction, but He has also promised to crown us with His loving kindness and tender mercies.

The truth of God's love surpasses any positive thinking or motivational encouragement that any man can provide.

Throughout my years of ministry, I have met many people who have never experienced the tender mercies of a father or the loving kindness of a parent. But when we give our lives to God, He is ready to shower us with His love and compassion.

This verse also means that He crowns us with His divine favor. I know people who are faithfully following the Lord, and who are surrounded with honor and favor beyond understanding. They are covered by God's kindness and mercy. This concept is an important truth that can destroy the roots and strongholds of rejection. The truth of God's love surpasses any positive thinking or motivational encouragement that any man can provide. We are no longer in need of doing everything within our power to gain acceptance from man. We already have acceptance from God. What great security we have in Him!

I don't think any of us can truly understand how much God loves us. From time to time, we can catch glimpses of it, and when we do, it makes our hearts soar. Think of it: He loved *you* so much that He sent His only begotten Son to die in your place! I am convinced that even if you were the only one who needed redemption—even if you were the only person who had ever sinned—He still would have sent His Son to die for you. As the Bible tells us, God is not willing that any should perish. His desire is for everyone to be saved and to spend eternity with Him. (See 2 Peter 3:9.)

5) GOD SATISFIES OUR MOUTHS WITH GOOD THINGS

This is the fifth of God's benefits that are listed in Psalm 103, and I believe it has at least three levels of interpretation: physical, mental and spiritual.

I have clung to this promise when I have been ministering overseas. Sometimes it is very very difficult to find food that is compatible with the American digestive system. Some-times it is difficult to find food that is compatible with American teeth! Some food is almost impossible—almost impossible to chew, almost impossible to swallow, and almost impossible to digest. But God has always provided good things for me to eat. I have always been satisfied and filled. God has satisfied my mouth with good things.

That's the physical part of this benefit.

In the mental and spiritual realms, this verse refers to the encouragement and edification that come through His goodness to us. When you have allowed God to be the Lord of your life, there is much good inside of you and it comes out of your mouth to bless others as well as yourself. Especially in times of stress and spiritual warfare, God will fill your mouth with encouraging songs, hymns and melodies that will bless and edify you.

Especially in times of stress and spiritual warfare, God will fill your mouth with encouraging songs, hymns and melodies that will bless and edify you.

For example, you may find yourself singing, "Oh, my God, I look unto you, from where my help will come. There is no evil that will overtake me because God is my deliverer." Words like these are more than just a confession of faith. They are borne out of the fact that the Spirit of the Lord is rising up within your spirit, giving you the songs that you need to overcome the challenges of life. I love it when I wake up in the morning and there is a song in my spirit, or when the pressures arise, but God's Spirit reacts to those pressures by filling my mouth with a song of triumph!

Now, let's take a look at the next benefit.

6) GOD RENEWS OUR YOUTH

One of the youngest men I know is a gentleman by the name of Lester Sumrall. Somebody says, "Now wait a minute! I know who Lester Sumrall is and he's got to be past 70." That's right, he is. But he has spent his life serving and loving God with all of his mind, heart and soul—and as a result he is a very young man in his spirit and in his approach to life, no matter what his chronological age may be.

But you know, some people are just the opposite of Lester Sumrall. They're not that old in years, but they are worn out and exhausted. They feel old and they act old. The pressures of the world have taken their toll. Now it is profitable for younger people to have the wisdom of the elderly, but it is not profitable for them to be tired and weary. If you have become weary, don't forget this benefit, which is God's promise of youthfulness for your physical body and your spirit.

Let me encourage you to allow the Spirit of God within you to rise up in you and heal the wounds that may be resident in your life. You will then learn to bless the Lord. Let your prayer be, "Lord, thank You for all Your benefits. Help me to never forget Your goodness. Give me the capacity to remember Your rescuing power and Your provision so that my youth may be renewed like the eagle's." (See Isaiah 40:31.)

The final benefit of God I'm going to discuss in this book is the seventh one to be found in Psalm 103.

7) GOD DELIVERS THE OPPRESSED

Are you oppressed? Are you under Satanic attack? Are you held down by worry, fear, financial difficulty, or an unreasonable and harsh boss? However it is that you are oppressed, God is willing and able to deliver you. He wants to deliver you!

When the Lord promises that He will execute righteousness and judgment for all who are oppressed, this promise applies to all those who are physically, mentally, or spiritually oppressed by the devil and his demonic hosts. Satan has no power over you if you belong to the Lord! Actively resist him and he will flee from you!

There are those in the world today who would attempt to silence the church. In our own government, we see more and more laws that are passed to restrict the activities of Christians. What these people don't understand is that God's laws are higher than man's laws. If man's laws and God's laws are in direct conflict, it is the laws of man that will be destroyed and not the other way around. God has given His church the right and the responsibility to declare what is morally correct.

Allow the Spirit of God within you to rise up in you and heal the wounds that may be resident in your life. You will then learn to bless the Lord.

Christians must always remember that God is on their side. He will not allow His people to be oppressed forever. Christians must always remember God's benefit of releasing His judgment and justice on those who try to oppress His church.

Remember…God has promised righteousness and judgment for all those who are oppressed.

Let's recap what we've talked about in this book:

+ We have discussed the importance of learning to bless the Lord.

- We have seen the importance of letting go of the past and moving ahead into the future.

- We have discovered that God provides these benefits for all who belong to him:

   1. Forgiveness of iniquities.

   2. Healing of diseases.

   3. Redemption from destruction.

   4. Crowning with loving kindness and tender mercies.

   5. Satisfying of the mouth with good things.

   6. Renewal of youth.

   7. Deliverance for the oppressed.

Christians must always remember
that God is on their side. He will not allow
His people to be oppressed forever.

May God bless and keep you as you walk in these truths!

DISCUSSION QUESTIONS:

1. How many of the benefits listed in Psalm 103 have you experienced?

2. What does it mean for you when the Bible says that God forgives all your iniquities?

3. What are some of the ways in which God has saved you from destruction?

4. What are some of the physical and spiritual blessings that God has provided in your life?

5. Name a time when God ministered to you in times of oppression.

ABOUT THE AUTHOR

ABOUT THE AUTHOR

Dr. Roberts Liardon is an author, public speaker, spiritual leader, church historian, and humanitarian. His mother was a charter class student at Oral Roberts University, Tulsa Oklahoma, at Roberts' birth. For the distinction of being the first male child born to an ORU student, his parents named him in honor of its founder, Oral Roberts.

Roberts was called into the ministry at a very young age. Kathryn Kuhlman prophesied to him as a young boy that he was called by God to serve in ministry to the church. Subsequently, he preached his first public sermon at the age of thirteen and began lecturing in Christian colleges and universities at age fifteen.

At sixteen, Roberts launched a radio program in Tulsa, and at seventeen, he wrote his first book, *I Saw Heaven*, which sold 1.5 million copies. This book was Roberts' account of his visit to heaven as an eight-year-old boy, and it catapulted Roberts into the public eye.

Shortly after the publication of *I Saw Heaven*, God inspired Roberts to write a bestselling book entitled *God's Generals*, which chronicled the lives and ministries of some of the leading Pentecostal and charismatic leaders. It would appear in both print and a video series. This achievement established Roberts as a leading Protestant church historian, a mantle he wears today.

The *God's Generals* series brought him international attention. Twice, he was awarded the prestigious title of "Outstanding Young Man of America." He met with former President Ronald Reagan, former Prime Minister Lady Margaret Thatcher, and Dr. Billy Graham. He has received letters of commendation from many others he has not met personally, including former President and first lady George and Laura Bush, honoring him for his commitment and contribution to improve the quality of life in his community.

In his mid-twenties, Roberts built one of the fastest growing churches in the U.S. and established his first accredited Bible college. From this ministry, he founded over forty churches, built five international Bible colleges, and assisted the poor and needy in his community, throughout America, and around the globe. He has sent close to five hundred humanitarian teams of men and women to various nations. These humanitarian teams not only share the Good News of Jesus Christ but also provide food, clothing, and medical assistance. In Namibia, Africa, Roberts helped to start the first HIV/AIDS prevention campaign in the public schools.

As he neared thirty, Roberts began a television program, *The High Life*, which was seen worldwide on the Trinity Broadcasting Network. Recently, he launched a new TV show called, *God's Generals with Roberts Liardon*, which is currently aired in more than two hundred countries.

Today, as a recognized church historian specializing in the Pentecostal and charismatic movements, Roberts has collected one of the world's largest collections of church history memorabilia. It contains rare books, films, photos, voice recordings, and personal effects of leaders of the Reformation as well as the Pentecostal and Charismatic movements.

Through the years, Roberts received spiritual oversight and personal mentorship from great men of God like Dr. Oral Roberts and Dr. Lester Sumrall. While still maintaining a demanding speaking schedule and writing new books, Roberts is mentoring a new generation of world leaders to effect change for the church and society.

Roberts continues to be an internationally best-selling author, having sold over seven million books in English alone, and his works have been translated into over fifty languages. His voice speaks to a current generation of believers who want to draw closer to the heart and mind of God and impact their communities and the nations of the world through the gospel of Jesus Christ.

Roberts Liardon Ministries

P.O. Box 2989 ✦ Sarasota, FL 34230

E-mail: info1@robertsliardon.org ✦ www. RobertsLiardon.com

Twitter: @RobertsLiardon ✦ Facebook: www. facebook.com/RobertsLiardon

Printed in Great Britain
by Amazon

42912472R00056